JOURNEY THROUGH
China

Philip Steele

Troll Associates

Library of Congress Cataloging-in-Publication Data

Steele, Philip, (date)
    Journey through China / by Philip Steele;
illustrated by Martin Camm, Mike Roffe,
Ian Thompson.
      p.   cm.
    Summary: An introduction to China, the
world's most populous country. Includes
a chart of key facts and information on
the population, language, and calendar.
    ISBN 0-8167-2112-2 (lib. bdg.)
    ISBN 0-8167-2113-0 (pbk.)
    1. China—Juvenile literature.
[1. China.] I. Camm, Martin, ill.
II. Roffe, Michael, ill. III. Thompson,
Ian, ill. IV. Title.
DS706.S774 1991
951—dc20   90-10943

This edition published in 2001.

Published by Troll Associates, Mahwah,
New Jersey 07430

Edited by Neil Morris

Design by James Marks
Picture research by Caroline Mitchell.

Illustrators: Martin Camm: pages 4, 5; Mike
Roffe: pages 5, 6-7, 8-9, 11, 14-15, 18, 25, 26-27;
Paul Sullivan: pages 16-17; Ian Thompson:
pages 4-5.

Picture Credits: Andes Press: page 21 (bottom);
Barnabys: pages 16, 24-25; Robert Harding: pages
14-15; Hutchison: pages 9 (top & bottom), 12-13,
13 (left & right), 15, 16-17, 18, 19 (bottom), 20, 22-23,
25, 27, 30 (top & bottom); Anderley Moore: cover,
pages 1, 22, 23; ZEFA: pages 6, 7, 10, 10-11, 19 (top),
21 (top), 26.

Printed in the U.S.A.
10   9   8   7   6   5

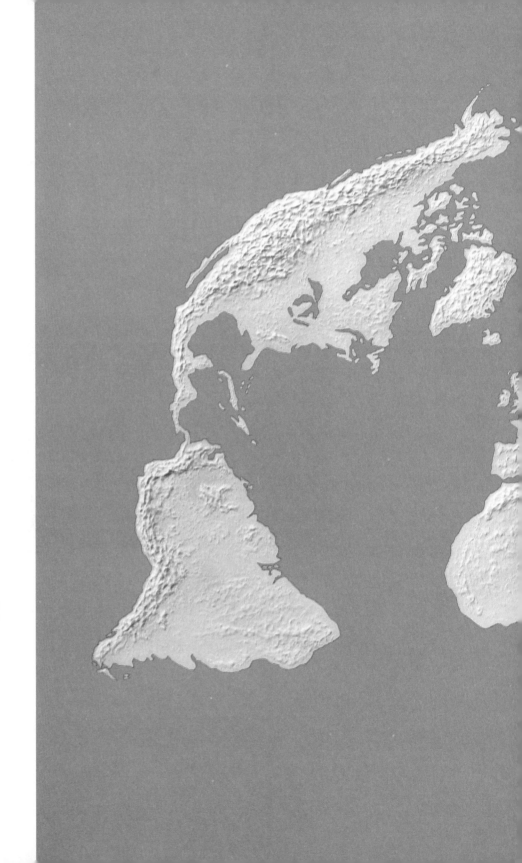

CONTENTS

People's Republic of China

Yak

Animals of China

The yak is a mountain ox that lives in the Himalayas. The giant panda lives in the bamboo forests of Sichuan. Cranes are marsh birds. Cranes and pandas are now very rare.

▼ In this book, we will take a journey through China. The numbers on the small map show which pages deal with which part of China.

Urumqi

T I E N   S H A N

XINJIANG

Kashi

T A K L I M A K A N   D E S E R T

G O B I   D E

I N N E R

NINGXIA

GREAT WALL

Altun Shan

Lake Qinghai

K u n l u n   S h a n

Huang He

Xi'an

TIBET
(XIZANG)

H i m a l a y a

Lhasa

Qomolongma (Mt. Everest) ▲

SICHUAN

Chengdu

Chongqing ●

Chang Jiang

GUIZHOU

● Kunming

GUANGXI

YUNNAN

14-15

8-13

18-19

16-17

20-21

24-25

22-23

26-27

Giant panda

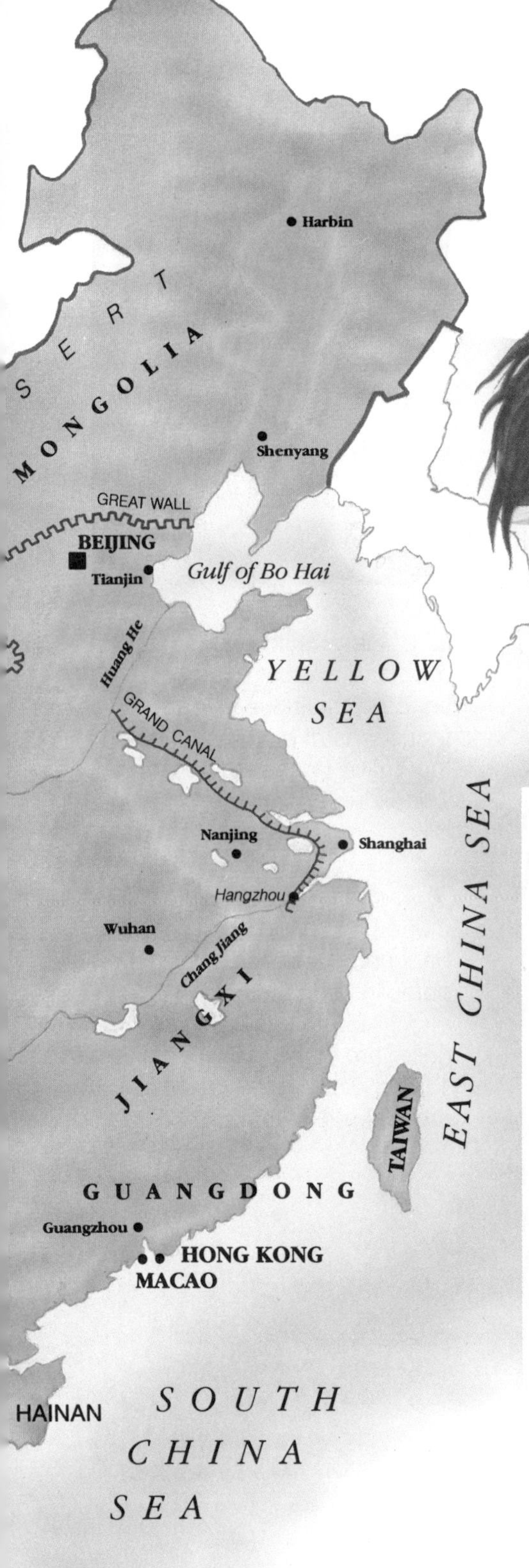

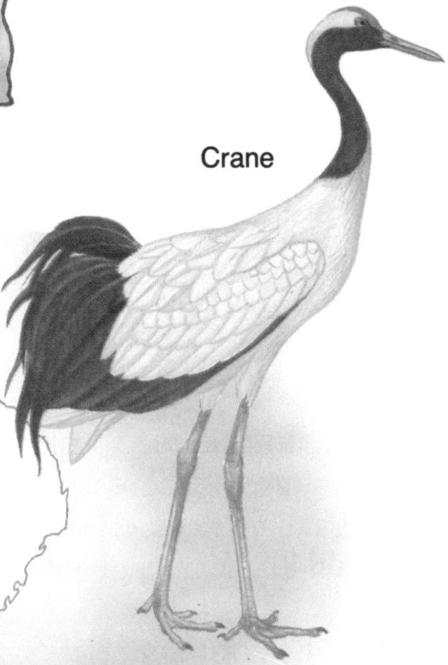

Crane

On the Chinese flag, the large star represents the Communist party. The four smaller stars represent the unity of the people – peasants, workers, soldiers, and students. The red background symbolizes the revolution that led to the founding of the People's Republic.

Map labels: DESERT, MONGOLIA, Harbin, Shenyang, GREAT WALL, BEIJING, Tianjin, Gulf of Bo Hai, Huang He, GRAND CANAL, YELLOW SEA, Nanjing, Shanghai, Hangzhou, Wuhan, Chang Jiang, JIANGXI, GUANGDONG, Guangzhou, HONG KONG, MACAO, TAIWAN, EAST CHINA SEA, HAINAN, SOUTH CHINA SEA

KEY FACTS

Area: 9,561,000 sq.km (3,692,000 sq. mi.) – the third biggest country in the world

Population: 1,100,000,000 – most people of any country in the world

Capital: Beijing (formerly Peking) 9,470,000 people

Other major cities: Shanghai 12,050,000 Tianjin 7,990,000 Chongqing 6,600,000

Highest mountain: Qomolongma (Mount Everest) 8,848 m (29,028 ft.) – world's highest

Longest rivers: Chang Jiang (Yangtze) 6,380 km (3,960 mi.) – the third longest river in the world Huang He (Yellow) about 5,000 km (3,100 mi.)

Largest lake: Qinghai 4,100 sq.km (1,660 sq. mi.)

5

Welcome to China

You can travel around China by plane, flying over high mountains and huge plains. You can bump along country roads in a bus or truck. You can rattle along in a steam train, or take a boat down one of China's great rivers. Most Chinese people ride bicycles, and that is certainly the best way to get around the big cities.

Wherever you go you will find a welcome. People will smile and say "*ni hao!*," which means "hello." Most people speak Mandarin Chinese, which is the official national language. In the south, people speak a different version of it, called Cantonese. There are many other languages too. No less than 56 different peoples live in China. Many have their own language, religion, dress, and way of life.

When you look at the signs in a bus or train station, you will see that Chinese is written in picture symbols. There are about 50,000 of these, so learning to write in China is hard work! A Chinese typewriter is complicated too. It has several trays of different symbols. Today, word processors make it easier to produce documents in Chinese. The Western way of writing Chinese, called *Pinyin*, is used for the Chinese words in this book.

At the station, people pay for their tickets in *renminbi*, or "people's money." Foreign visitors use special banknotes called "foreign exchange certificates."

Traveling around China takes a long time, but it is very exciting. The country is about the size of the whole continent of Europe. It stretches from the snowy plains of Russia to the steamy jungles of Vietnam. Over 1 billion people live in China, which is more than in any other country in the world.

▲ Chinese children learn to read and write at primary school. They have to learn the thousands of picture symbols that make up the Chinese written language.

▼ *Renminbi*, the "people's money," is made up of banknotes and coins. Large notes include those for 10, 5, and 1 *yuan*. Medium-sized notes are in *jiao*. 10 jiao make 1 yuan. Small notes and coins are in *fen*. 10 fen make 1 jiao.

▲ All China's cities have large bicycle parks, with attendants to look after them.

China's capital city

China's capital city is Beijing. On old maps it is often written as Peking. Many foreign visitors arrive at Beijing airport, or at the bustling central train station. The Trans-Siberian express comes here all the way from Moscow. The train journey takes six days.

The Beijing area is home to nine million people. In the center of the city is the world's biggest public square. Here you may see excited children flying kites or buying ice cream. At one end of the square is an ancient building called Tiananmen, the Gate of Heavenly Peace.

On Tiananmen Gate is a huge picture of the Chinese leader Mao Zedong, who lived from 1893 to 1976. Mao was a Communist. He believed that working people and peasants should run the country, rather than landowners and rich business people. Mao spent much of his life fighting Japanese soldiers who had invaded his country. He also fought Jiang Jieshi (Chiang Kai-shek) and the Chinese Nationalists, who were against Communism. By 1949 the Communists had beaten both the Japanese and the Nationalists. Mao stood at Tiananmen Gate and declared China a People's Republic. The Nationalists fled to the island of Taiwan. There, they set up their own government.

China is still a Communist country, but it has gone through many changes. Today, foreign business people are welcome in China. In the center of Beijing there are large advertisements for Japanese and American goods.

In 1989 thousands of people marched through Beijing and gathered in Tiananmen Square. They wanted Chinese leaders to change the way the country is run. The leaders refused, and sent soldiers in against the protesters. Many people were killed.

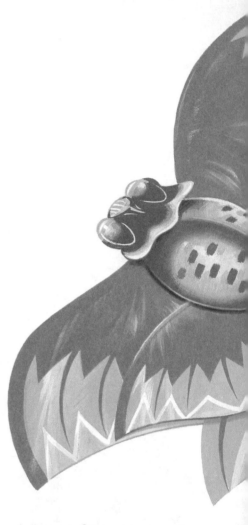

▲ In every Chinese town and city you will see people flying kites. Children may fly home-made kites or buy cheap, colorful ones made of tissue paper. Sometimes the kites become tangled in the branches of trees. Some grownups fly kites as a hobby. They may make kites which look like dragons or flocks of doves.

▲ Schoolchildren visit Tiananmen Gate in the center of Beijing. The big picture is of Mao Zedong, who founded the People's Republic.

◀ Opera in the Beijing style is popular throughout China. The actors who play villains paint their faces with colored patterns. The heroes and heroines have more simple make-up. The actors mime and sing to the music of a small Chinese orchestra. The plots are well known and much loved. When Mao was alive, modern operas were performed. These told stories about workers, soldiers, and peasants.

Journey into history

When you pass through Tiananmen Gate, you come to the magnificent Imperial Palace. This was the home of the emperors who ruled China long ago. It was surrounded by a moat and high walls, and the common people were not allowed to enter. Today, the so-called Forbidden City is open to everyone.

Each year, the emperor used to lead a procession from the Forbidden City to the Temple of Heaven. The people were not allowed to see the emperor and had to hide behind closed doors as he passed by with his courtiers and soldiers.

For hundreds of years, China was the most advanced civilization in the world. Paper, printing,

▼ Chinese emperors were once crowned in the Hall of Supreme Harmony, in Beijing's Forbidden City.

▶ This part of the Great Wall is 70 kilometers (44 miles) from Beijing. It failed to stop invasions from the north.

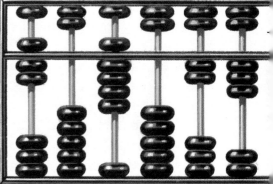

silk, fine pottery, the compass, and banknotes were all invented in China. Chinese mathematicians were among the first to use the decimal system. A wooden frame called an *abacus* is still used for working out sums. Some people do arithmetic with it as quickly as on an electronic calculator!

The Chinese empire was defended from attack by a huge wall across the north of the country. The Great Wall still stands. It stretches for nearly 6,700 kilometers (4,100 miles), crossing mountains and valleys. It can even be seen from the moon! You can take a bus from Beijing and visit parts of the wall that have been restored. As you shiver in the cold wind, you can imagine what it was like to be a Chinese soldier long ago, waiting for fierce warriors to ride down and attack the wall.

▲ A Chinese abacus has 9, 11, or 13 rods in the frame. On the six rods you can see, each has two beads above the bar, and five below. Each bead above the bar is worth five of the beads below. Each lower bead is worth 10 times the bead on its right. The figure shown here is 709,023.

Modern city life

Modern Beijing has broad avenues lined with stores, hospitals, and restaurants. Narrow lanes lead off the main streets. They are usually crowded with shoppers buying fruit and vegetables, or with people pushing bicycles loaded high with packages.

Most city dwellers live in apartments. These are often quite crowded, as China is still a fairly poor country. But the housing is far better than it was 50 years ago, when many people lived in misery. Because China is so crowded, married couples are encouraged to have only one child.

Many children wear the red scarf of the Young Pioneers, who are like boy scouts and girl scouts. Toddlers go to nursery school, or are cared for by their grandparents while their parents go out to work. At the age of six or seven, children go to primary school. They learn to read and write, and study science, math, art, history, geography, and physical education. At the age of 13, many children move up to secondary school, where they may study for three to five years. At 16 to 18, they may go on to universities or technical colleges.

Young Chinese like to play football, basketball, billiards, and table tennis, and enjoy swimming. Smaller children like to make and fly kites, while older children are more interested in pop music and discos. They also enjoy watching kung fu films on television. Kung fu is a form of exercise and self-defense first practiced by monks in ancient China. Many other martial arts are also popular. Some involve swordplay, while others are based on boxing.

Older people prefer a more relaxed exercise called taijiquan. Every morning hundreds of them gather in Beijing's parks to practice the rhythmic movements of taijiquan.

▲ A parade in Beijing marks Children's Day, June 1st. Chinese grownups make a great fuss of young children. This may be because city families are expected to have just one child each.

▶ Ping pong, or table tennis, is often played on city streets and in parks. The Chinese are good table tennis players. They have won gold medals in the sport at the Olympic Games.

▼ Men practice taijiquan in Beijing's Temple of Heaven park. City parks are lively places. People relax by playing cards, practicing sports, or doing exercises.

Manchus and Mongols

Beijing lies in the northeast of China. The provinces bordered by Korea and eastern Russia were formerly known as Manchuria. The Manchus were a people who conquered China in the 1600s and ruled for nearly 300 years.

The quickest train from Beijing to the northern town of Harbin takes 17 hours. So it is worth taking a "soft seat," which means you will travel in comfort. The "hard seat" sections of Chinese trains are cheaper, more crowded, noisy, and much less comfortable.

In winter the temperature in the northern provinces can fall to −30°C (−22°F). Milk is then sold in frozen bricks, and meat is wrapped in dough, frozen, and preserved.

The central north of China is called Inner Mongolia. The region once known as Outer Mongolia is now a separate country, the Mongolian People's Republic. The open grasslands of Inner Mongolia stretch all the way to the Gobi Desert.

▲ Mongolian cooking requires special stewing pots. These are made at factories in China and exported around the world. The pots keep stock simmering at the table, so that pieces of meat and vegetables may be dipped in.

▲ Many of the people of Inner Mongolia follow the old way of life. They round up their herds on horseback.

The Mongols are expert horseback riders who follow their herds across the grasslands. Some still live in traditional round tents made of felt, called yurts. Others have settled in towns and villages. Mongols follow the Buddhist religion and have their own language, laws, and customs.

Over 700 years ago a Mongol leader named Genghis Khan conquered lands all the way to Europe. The Mongols went on to rule China itself.

◄ You can still see giant steam locomotives in China.

15

The Yellow River

A great river rises in China's western mountains and winds through the plains of northern China to the sea. It is called the Huang He, which means Yellow River, and it is about 5,000 kilometers (3,100 miles) long. Its waters are colored with yellowish-brown mud, washed from the banks. Over the ages, the Huang He has changed its course many times. Floods have drowned farms and villages, causing great hardship. Today the floods are partly controlled by dams, but these are often clogged up with mud.

The soil around the Huang He is rich and ideal for farming. Because China has so many mouths to feed, every bit of farming land must be used. Trees are planted to stop soil from being blown away.

▲ Flooding is a problem on the Huang He. Dikes and dams have been dug to control the muddy waters.

◀ Soldiers of the terra cotta army. The statues were dug from the tomb of the first Chinese emperor.

▶ The rich soil of the Huang He is ideal for farming. Many farmers plow with a simple "walking" tractor. Crops include wheat, millet, and fruit such as pears.

Bayan Har Mountains

It was on this rich farming land that Chinese civilization first began, about 9,000 years ago. Today, you can visit an ancient village that has been dug out of the soil at Banpo, near the city of Xi'an. It is about 7,000 years old, and includes the ruins of houses, kilns for baking pottery, and a burial ground.

If you take a bus eastwards from Xi'an, you come to another amazing sight. Here is an army of over 6,000 life-size statues of soldiers, horses, and chariots. They are made of terra cotta, or earthenware. They were put on guard around the tomb of Qin Shi Huangdi, the first emperor to rule a united China, over 2,000 years ago. This ghostly army was discovered five meters (16 feet) underground.

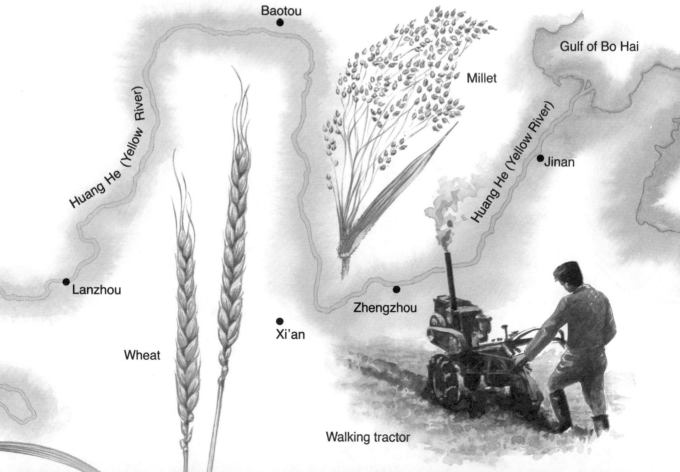

Baotou

Gulf of Bo Hai

Millet

Huang He (Yellow River)

Huang He (Yellow River)

Jinan

Lanzhou

Zhengzhou

Wheat

Xi'an

Walking tractor

Across the wilderness

▲ Followers of Islam are called to prayer five times a day. This mosque is in Kashi, in China's far west.

▼ It takes a truck between three and four days to travel from Urumqi to Kashi.

The northwest of China is a land of bleak mountains and stony wastes. One desert is called the Taklimakan, which means "go in, and you won't come out again!" Towns and industries have sprung up here because the harsh landscape contains mineral riches.

The largest town is Urumqi. Here the people speak languages that sound like Turkish. They are the Uygurs, Tajiks, and Uzbeks. Their religion is Islam, and they worship in mosques.

Islam came to China from the Middle East. Merchants from Arabia and Persia passed through the northwest with their camels and pack horses. Their most precious load was fine silk, woven from the cocoons of Chinese silkworms. Today, buses and trucks take the new Karakoram Highway to Pakistan.

To the south lies the region of Xizang, which we know as Tibet. Tibet is a lonely, beautiful wilderness perched among the world's highest mountains. Mount Everest, or Qomolongma, is the world's highest peak, at 8,848 meters (29,028 feet). It is part of the Himalaya range, on the border between Tibet and Nepal. You can fly over the mountain ranges to the city of Lhasa, the Tibetan capital.

The Tibetans are Buddhists, and have their own language and way of life. For many years, the world knew little of this remote mountain country. Some Tibetans live by herding large, shaggy mountain oxen called yaks. Yak milk is used to make sour butter, which is served in tea.

▲ The Potala Palace towers above the city of Lhasa.

▼ In Tibet, Buddhism developed its own forms of worship.

19

Boat down the Chang Jiang

Sichuan province borders on Tibet. It is a land of mountains and misty forests. Dense thickets of bamboo grow in the west, which are home to the giant panda.

The capital of Sichuan is Chengdu. Its broad avenues are lined with modern buildings. Here you can stop at a teahouse or eat a meal of rice with peanuts and pork. The local cooking is very spicy with lots of garlic and chili.

Sichuan's rivers flow into the Chang Jiang, which means "long river." It is also called the Yangtze. It is nearly 6,400 kilometers (4,000 miles) long, which makes it the world's third longest river.

The Chang Jiang is busy with barges and small boats. You can take a four-decker riverboat

▶ The Shanghai skyline at night. The city was built as a center of foreign trade on the Huang Pu river, which flows into the Chang Jiang.

▼ A riverboat tackles the strong currents of the Chang Jiang. Rivers are often used for transport in China. Boats like this carry large numbers of passengers. They travel from Chongqing to big river ports such as Wuhan.

downstream from the city of Chongqing. All sorts of passengers take the boat. There are tourists, soldiers, and farmers with chickens clucking in wicker baskets. The boat leaves the gray hills behind at dawn and follows the river eastward past villages and towns. Soon the river is rushing through deep mountain gorges. The power of the current is used to make electricity at the massive Gezhouba Dam. Below the dam, the river is wide and slow.

After five days on the riverboat, you arrive in Shanghai. Here the Chang Jiang flows into the East China Sea. Over 12 million people live in Shanghai, which is China's largest city and a center of shipping and industry. The old quarter is a maze of narrow alleys. It is so overcrowded that homework, Chinese chess, cooking, and even family quarrels often take place in the street.

▼ Boats traveling down the Chang Jiang enter a lock at the Gezhouba Dam. The dam provides electricity. It is one of China's greatest energy projects.

To the land of spring

The train journey from Shanghai to Kunming, capital of Yunnan province, takes many days. You can fly there by airplane in only three hours. Here in Kunming, the climate is spring-like for most of the year. Traders sell watermelons and pineapples in the tree-lined streets, and the city parks are bright with marigolds and poppies.

You may see people selling medicines in the street. Many of these are made from roots and herbs. Although China has modern hospitals and medicines, some people prefer more traditional methods of healing. One traditional Chinese medical treatment is acupuncture. Needles are stuck into the body to cure illness or relieve pain. This does not hurt the patient!

Beautiful countryside attracts many tourists to Yunnan and to the nearby provinces of Guizhou and Guangxi. There are blue lakes for fishing, and hazy mountains for climbing. At Shillin, limestone rocks form tall pillars in amazing shapes. A plane ride south to the Burmese border brings you to lush tropical forests.

The main crop of southern China is rice. Seedlings are planted in flooded fields, which are plowed by water buffalo. When the plants have grown and ripened, the fields are drained so that the rice can be harvested.

Rice is beaten, or threshed, in the local village. Village houses are often made of clay bricks and roofed with tiles or thatch. Pigs and chickens wander the dusty streets. Cooking is often done on an outside stove.

▶ A Chinese soldier buys fresh greens at a street market in Yunnan.

22

▲ Women plant rice in flooded fields near China's border with Burma. They wear straw hats to protect them from the hot sun. Rice is China's main food, and millions of tons of it must be produced each year to feed the vast population.

▶ This little piggy went to market on the back of a bicycle, all bound up in wicker.

Ferries, junks, and barges

Three rivers make up the Zhujiang waterway, which starts in Yunnan and flows into the South China Sea in Guangdong province. The central part of southern China is hot and moist. Sometimes, fierce tropical storms called typhoons lash the coast, and fishing boats have to stay in harbor.

Guangzhou, once known as Canton, is the great port of southern China. It is a huge city, filled with traffic, markets, and fashionably dressed crowds. Cantonese cooking is famous all over the world. Fish, pork, and chicken are favorites, and you will find snake and sea slug on the menu too!

There are many factories around Guangzhou. Chemicals, foodstuffs, and modern electronic equipment are produced here. Trade fairs are held in the city.

From Guangzhou you can take a ferry to Hainan island. You may pass large ships and traditional wooden boats called junks. Sharks and flying fish live in these waters. Hainan has a tropical climate, and beautiful beaches.

During the age of the emperors, Jiangxi province was famous for its white clay, which was made into fine pottery known as porcelain. Chinese porcelain (or china) is still treasured all over the world. Today, coal and steel are also produced in Jiangxi.

The city of Hangzhou is on the Grand Canal. The engineering of this great waterway was carried out between 400 B.C. and A.D. 1327. At one time about five million laborers were working on just one section. The Grand Canal was built to link Hangzhou and the farmlands of the south with Beijing. Barges carried rice and other goods northwards. Over the ages the canal became clogged up with mud, but today much of it has been reopened for shipping.

▶ A boat full of produce floats down the Grand Canal. Scenes like this have been common for hundreds of years.

▼ Once, large wooden ships called junks were a common sight in the South China Sea. The Chinese were the first to build ships with several masts and with underwater rudders for steering.

▲ Chopsticks are really quite easy to use. One stick is held between the thumb and the base of the first two fingers. The other is supported by the third finger. Both chopsticks should be held near the top.

China around the world

Many visitors to China come and go through Hong Kong, an island off the coast of Guangdong province. Hong Kong is a center of manufacture and trade. The hovercraft from Guangzhou takes three hours. When you arrive, you will see big ships at anchor, and towering skyscrapers.

The people of Hong Kong speak Cantonese. The city is very crowded and many poor families live on small boats called sampans.

To the east, the large island of Taiwan is a separate country, ruled by the Chinese Nationalists. The people from Taiwan are free to travel in China, and many come to visit their relatives on the mainland.

▲ A hydrofoil speeds from Hong Kong. Many visitors enter mainland China from here, on boats, trains, or planes.

◄ In Hong Kong, boats are used for travel, and also for living in. Sheltered harbors are built to protect ships from the violent tropical storms called typhoons.

► Dragon dancers weave their way through Beijing. The same sight could well be seen during Chinese New Year in London, San Francisco, or Sydney. The Chinese way of life is now familiar to people all over the world.

It is sad to leave China and the new friends you have made. But you are sure to meet Chinese people wherever you travel in the world. Over the years, many have settled in Europe, America, Australia, and Southeast Asia. Some have kept their own language and customs.

The Chinese New Year is celebrated all over the world. It is a time for family gatherings and parties. Fireworks are set off and lines of dancers, huddled under long dragon costumes, weave through the crowds in the street. The aim of the festival is to bring good luck for the future.

Fact file

The language of China

The Chinese language has many different spoken dialects. But the written symbols that represent the words are the same throughout China. Thousands of years ago, each symbol, or character, was based on a picture. Gradually these pictures became simple brushstrokes.

The tone used to say a word can change its meaning completely: *mao* means *cat*, *hat,* or *spear*, depending on how it is spoken!

Mandarin Chinese is spoken by about 747 million people. It is the most spoken language in the world.

Say it in Chinese!

	Character	Mandarin Chinese	how to say it
hello	你好	ni hao	nee-how
goodbye	再見	zaijian	dzie-jiahn
China	中國	Zhongguo	jawng-gwaw
thank you	謝謝	xiexie	zhyeh-zhyeh
one	一	yi	yee
two	二	er	ur
three	三	san	sahn

Borders

China has more borders than any other country in the world. It borders on 14 countries. Starting at North Korea and going clockwise, they are: North Korea, Vietnam, Laos, Myanmar, India, Bhutan, (India again), Nepal, (India again), Pakistan, Afghanistan, Tajikistan, Kyrgyzstan, Kazakhstan, Russia, Mongolia, (Russia again). These borders stretch for 24,000 km (15,000 mi).

Coastline

China's coastline is over 18,000 km (11,000 mi.) long. It stretches along the Gulf of Bo Hai, the Yellow Sea, and the East and South China Seas. Off the coast there are over 5,000 islands. Apart from nationalist Taiwan, the largest island is Hainan. Many of China's islands are tiny coral reefs in warm tropical waters.

Population

About 12.8 million babies are born in China each year. The population for 1990 was estimated to be 1,100 million. Parents are encouraged to have only one child.

Land of the bicycle

There are over 130 million bicycles in China. 30 million new bikes are produced each year!

The Chinese calendar

In China, each year is named after an animal. There are 12 different animals, and people born in each year are supposed to share the character of that year's animal. Which animal are you? Look for your year of birth below, then see what your animal represents.

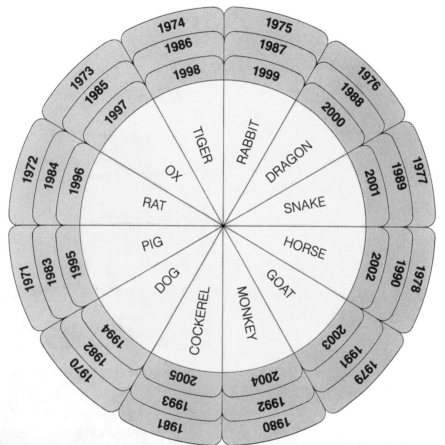

Rabbits are quiet, peaceful, and successful.
Dragons are lucky, full of energy, and know what they want in life.
Snakes are wise, and often keep secrets.
Horses look for success and lively company, and love fashion and travel.
Goats like art, and are often perfectionists.
Monkeys are clever and cunning, especially when it comes to making money.
Cockerels are intelligent and efficient.
Dogs are loyal and kind.
Pigs are popular and like a laugh.
Rats are friendly and sociable.
Oxen are serious and quiet, but can be stubborn and even lose their temper.
Tigers are lucky, adventurous, and daring.

First printers and papers

The art of papermaking and printing from wooden blocks was invented in China nearly 2,000 years ago. Court circulars were published under the reign of Emperor Ming (A.D. 713-741).

A huge encyclopedia was written in China nearly 600 years ago. It was made up of more than 11,000 volumes.

Railways

There are 52,500 km (32,600 mi.) of railways in China. Some stretches are electrified, but steam trains are still widely used.

Farming

More than two thirds of Chinese workers are employed in farming. The main products are rice, wheat, cotton, silk, tobacco, peanuts, and fruit.

China is the world's top producer of rice, cotton, and tobacco.

Religions

Three main religions were followed in ancient China. *Confucianism* and *Taoism* were based on the sayings of wise men who lived in China over 2,500 years ago. *Buddhism* came to China from India about 2,000 years ago.

Peoples

Over 93 per cent of the people of China are Han Chinese. The name comes from the Han dynasty, which ruled China from 206 B.C. to A.D. 220. The remaining 7 per cent – at least 70 million people! – belong to one of 56 other ethnic groups. The largest minority groups are the Zhuang (12 million), the Hui (6.5 million), and the Miao (4 million).

▶ The women (*above*) are Buddhists, and belong to the Tu people. The man (*opposite*) is Muslim, and belongs to the Uygur people.

B.C.	Time chart
600,000	Prehistoric human beings live in China.
7000	Beginnings of civilization in the Yellow River valley. Stone weapons and tools.
2100	Rulers of the Xia take power.
1766	China ruled by Shang warriors. Bronze weapons. Silk making.
c 1122	Zhou warriors from the north conquer Shang.
c 640	Lao Zi is born. His ideas form the Taoist religion.
551	Confucius (Kong Fuzi) is born. His ideas form the Confucian religion.
400	Work begins on the Grand Canal.
246	Major building work begins on the Great Wall.
221	Qin Shi Huangdi, the first emperor, rules over a united China from the city of Xi'an.
206	The Han people seize power. The Buddhist religion becomes accepted in China.
A.D.	
220	Civil wars. China splits into three kingdoms.
618	T'ang emperors rule China. They bring prosperity and trade.
907	Peasant uprisings and civil wars.
960	Unity under the Sung emperors.
1217	Mongols attack China. Genghis Khan captures Beijing.
1271	Kublai Khan rules China from Beijing.
1368	Southerners (the Ming) seize power.
1421	The emperor's court moves to the Forbidden City, Beijing.
1644	Manchus (the Qing) seize power.

1839	War with British over opium trading.
1851	Taiping rebellion against the Manchus.
1862	Power passes to the Manchu emperor's widow, Cixi.
1900	Rebellion by Boxers ("Society of Righteous and Harmonious Fists") against foreign powers trading in China.
1911	End of Manchu rule. China becomes a republic.
1921	Chinese Communist party founded.
1931	Japanese invade Manchuria.
1949	Mao Zedong founds Communist People's Republic of China. The Nationalists flee to Taiwan.
1958	"Great Leap Forward" unsuccessful program by Mao to improve production in industry. People's communes set up.
1960	China quarrels with its chief ally, the Soviet Union.
1966	Cultural Revolution, started by Mao to prevent rise of ruling class.
1971	China becomes a member of the United Nations.
1972	U.S. President Nixon visits China.
1976	Death of Mao Zedong. Deng Xiaoping comes to power. China opens to the outside world.
1979	Full diplomatic relations with the U.S.A.
1989	Students demand reform. Troops kill protesters in Beijing.
1997	Hong Kong returned to Chinese on July 1.
1999	Macao returned to Chinese on December 20.

Index